POWER
SWING
IN 15 DAYS

Also by the authors

Break 100 in 21 Days:
A How-to Guide for the Weekend Golfer

Correct the 10 Most Common Golf Problems in 10 Days

Two-Putt Greens in 18 Days:
A How-to Guide for the Weekend Golfer

POWER SWING

IN **15** DAYS

A How-to Guide for the Weekend Golfer

WALTER OSTROSKE
PGA Teaching Pro

and JOHN DEVANEY

Photography by Aime J. LaMontagne

A PERIGEE BOOK

Perigee Books
are published by
The Putnam Publishing Group
200 Madison Avenue
New York, NY 10016

Library of Congress Cataloging-in-Publication Data

Ostroske, Walter.
    Power swing in 15 days : a how-to guide for the weekend golfer /
    Walter Ostroske and John Devaney ; photography by Aime LaMontagne.
        p.   cm.
    "A Perigee book."
    ISBN 0-399-51797-9
    1. Swing (Golf)   I. Devaney, John.   II. Title.
GV979.S9088   1993   92-35956   CIP
796.352'3—dc20

Cover design by Richard Rossiter
Cover photo by Aime J. LaMontagne

Printed in the United States of America
1   2   3   4   5   6   7   8   9   10

This book is printed on acid-free paper.

This book is dedicated to my late father, Walter Sr., who got me started in golf.

Contents

So You Want To Be a Power Golfer 9

DAY ONE: The Power Stance and Grip 13

DAY TWO: The Power Upswing 19

DAY THREE: The Power Downswing 28

DAY FOUR: The Late, Late Power Release 39

DAY FIVE: The Power Impact and Follow-Through 49

DAY SIX: The Lower-Gear Action for Super Power 58

DAY SEVEN: The Power Swing With Fairway Woods 70

DAY EIGHT: The Power Swing With Long Irons 75

DAY NINE: The Power Swing With Medium Irons 81

DAY TEN: The Power Swing With Short Irons 87

DAY ELEVEN: Power Your Way Out of Trouble 93

DAY TWELVE: Course Management for the Power Golfer 104

DAY THIRTEEN: At the Pro Shop: Equipment for Power Golf 109

DAY FOURTEEN: How to Practice for Power 117

DAY FIFTEEN: The Keys to Power Golf 121

So You Want To Be a Power Golfer

This happens to perhaps one of every two weekenders who come to me for lessons: After 21 days of lessons like those in my book *Break 100 in 21 Days*, the weekender is taking a nice, easy and comfortable swing. He or she drives the ball off the tee 170 to 185 yards. A fairway wood or an iron shot of about 150 yards puts the weekender close enough for an approach shot to the green. More often than not, the golfer lands on the green no more than one or two strokes over regulation. This kind of golfer will break 100 about three of every 10 rounds he or she plays.

Walter Ostroske: In 15 days I'll teach you how to hit longer off the tee and off the fairway.

But golfers are forever unhappy with their game—and scores. "I'm playing OK, Walter," my weekend player will tell me. "But I really would love to hit the ball longer."

Who wouldn't? I average 250 yards off the tee—and I would love to hit that little white rascal out there 300 yards.

"I'll teach you in 15 days of lessons to hit longer off the tee and off the fairway," I tell those players, most of whom are high-handicappers. They play once or twice a week during the season and average between 95 and 110.

It's important that they play reasonably often to build up the wrist and forearm strength needed to play power golf. But you don't need the muscles of a weight lifter. "I can teach you how to hit 200 yards or longer with your driver," I promise golfers, "whether you're a 250-pound linebacker or a 110-pound model."

I point out that Chi Chi Rodriguez has proven that even a skinny, 150-pound man can belt a ball 240 yards, and dozens of lady pros have proven the same thing to women. I tell my weekend players: "If you're averaging 175 yards with your driver, we'll get you up to 190 and maybe close to 200 yards in 15 days. And if you have been using a five-iron to go 150 yards on the fairway, I'll teach you how to hit the ball longer on those approach shots, so that you can go down a club and cover those same 150 yards with a six-iron."

"That's great," they tell me, "because I'd rather swing a shorter iron, like the number six, if I can get the same distance with it that I used to get with the longer number five."

"Of course you would," I say. "You can make a mistake with a shorter iron and your shot won't go off course as far as it would if you made the same mistake with a longer iron. The shorter the club, the more forgiving the club."

"Then show me how I can hit longer," they tell me.

"Whoa!" I say. "First you've got to accept three things that go with power golf."

"What three things?"

"First, be willing to go to the driving range and practice for a half hour to an hour what I teach you during each of the 15 lessons. Or at least swing at those plastic practice balls in your backyard or the basement for a half hour to an hour a day.

"Second, you must accept some loss of accuracy. You'll be hitting the ball longer—but you are not going to be hitting the ball as often to the safe places where you've been landing up to now. People who hit long will end up in trouble—rough, trees, out of bounds—a good deal more often than people who hit short. That's a fact of golf. However, we can work together to keep those wild shots to a minimum."

Most golfers are willing to make that trade-off: The joy they get out of booming a long drive that lands 50 yards past their partner's ball makes up for occasional trips into the woods to look for a lost ball.

"Third," I tell them, "you must build up strength in what I call your Golf Connection—your fingers, hands and forearms, which connect the club to your body. Each day I am going to give you easy, simple, no-sweat exercises to strengthen your hands, wrists and forearms. They are exercises that you can do while watching TV or sitting in an office. But by the end of the day you will have had a golf workout. And because it's a workout that's simple, easy, comfortable and fun, you'll do it the next day and the next."

To sum up: If you are willing to practice, if you are willing to shrug off the occasional wild shot, and if you are willing to build up your Golf Connection over the next 15 days, then you're ready to get started. Let's make you a long hitter and, just as important, an accurate hitter.

DAY ONE

The Power Stance and Grip

THE STANCE

You are standing at the tee and looking toward a green maybe 300 yards away. More often than not, you are thinking, "I want to slam this little white rascal so hard that it will never stop rolling."

So what do you do to gain more power and stretch that drive? You widen your stance. Instead of setting your feet so that they line up with your shoulders, you set your feet so they extend beyond the width of your shoulders. Most golfers equate a wider stance with more power. In reality, the reverse is true. To get more power, take a slightly narrower stance, so that your feet are inside your shoulder line.

Why?

A slightly narrower stance will allow more room for the body to turn and coil. A wider stance allows less room for the body to turn and coil, both on the backswing and—at the other end—on the follow-through. When a golfer takes a wider stance, the body can turn

For the power stance, keep the feet inside the shoulders.

only to the point where the width of the stance gets in the way of the body. As a result, the takeaway is shorter than the takeaway in the normal, shoulder-width stance. When the stance is narrower, you have an easier and better point for the body to pivot around. The hips and shoulders can turn to a fuller degree on both the backswing and the follow-through. The fuller the turn, the wider the swing arc and the longer the extension of the arms. A wide arc and a full extension of the arms—on both takeaway and follow-through—produce more clubhead speed. And clubhead speed is the name of the game in power golf.

Your stance, then, is slightly narrower than the one you have been using. The feet are inside the shoulder line, with the back foot drawn back slightly from the front to give better balance.

THE GRIP

Normally, you grip the club so that the thumbs of both hands run straight down the shaft, the palms of both hands facing each other. For a power grip, turn the left or the right hand—or both hands—slightly to the right. This is called a "strong" grip, whether it is strong in the left hand, the right hand or in both hands.

Since the dominant hand on the club should be the left hand, I recommend that you turn only the left hand more to the right side (see photo page 16). This will give the left hand more power or "push" than you would get with a normal grip. That left-hand push, just before impact, will ensure more clubhead speed.

The advantage of a strong grip over a normal grip is that you will get more of your hand strength into the

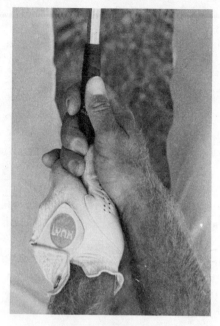

A golfer's view looking down at the normal grip.

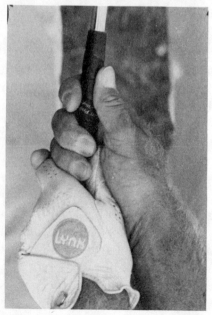

A golfer's view looking down at the power grip.

swing at impact. The disadvantage of a strong grip is that you are more likely to impart a hook spin to the ball, causing it to veer right to left. (I will explain how to avoid hooking with the stronger grip when I get to the downswing during Day Three.)

To sum up today's lesson, your setup for the power swing differs from the setup for your normal swing in only two ways: (1) You take a narrower stance, and (2) you use a strong grip by turning the left hand a few inches more to the right side.

Drills for the Power Stance and Power Grip

1. For 15 to 30 minutes, practice gripping and ungripping a club using the left-hand power grip. Each time you grip the club, check the position of your fingers and thumbs in a mirror to make sure you are gripping the club as I am gripping it in the photo at the bottom of page 16. During the next 15 days, grip and ungrip a club for five to ten minutes a day, always checking in a mirror to make sure the grip is correct.

2. Take the power stance, feet inside the shoulders, and swing a club for 15 to 30 minutes. You can swing at balls, real ones or plastic ones, or you can swing at an imaginary ball. Do this for a few minutes each day during the next 15 days.

Exercises for the Golf Connection

Sit in a chair that has arms. Extend your wrists and hands so they flap over the arms of the chair. Ball your hands into fists. Lift your fists up and down 40 or 50

17

times. This isometric exercise uses tension to build strength. You can do this exercise anytime you sit down in a chair with arms.

Sitting at a table or a desk, place your fingers under the table or desk and try to raise it. Even if the table or desk is too heavy to lift, you'll exert enough fingertip pressure to strengthen the wrists and forearms. Do this at least 50 times.

The Power Upswing

Picture yourself holding a bow and arrow like Robin Hood. You want to shoot the arrow so it zips to its target. You set the arrow in the bow string. You draw back the string until the taut string is almost touching your nose. You let go of the string—and the arrow flies to the target.

Now you put a second arrow in the string and draw it back. You keep pulling back the string until it is almost touching your ear. You let go of the string. The arrow flies to the target.

Which arrow flew faster—the first or the second?

The second flew faster because the string's tension was greater when you drew the string back past your nose to your ear. You extended the arc of the bow's string.

Extension.

That's the key word for you to remember in today's lesson—the fullest possible extension of the arms during the upswing. If you extend the arms and the hands as wide and as high as possible on the upswing, you are widening the arc of the swing path. The wider the arc, the faster the clubhead will travel on its downward path to impact. And the faster the clubhead is traveling at impact, the greater distance the ball will fly.

Extending the arc of a bow's string adds power to the arrow.

Let's go to a practice tee either at a driving range or in your backyard or basement. Take a slightly narrower stance and move your left hand slightly to the right to assume a strong grip.

Begin the takeaway. Bring the club away slowly, perhaps at half the speed you normally bring away the club. You want to bring the club away slowly so that you have the time to make sure that the width and height of the swing arc is going to be fully extended.

Get the fullest possible extension of the arms during the upswing.

At the top of the upswing, the clubhead is parallel to the ground or even below parallel. Most of your weight is on the right leg, with the left heel off the ground.

Again, *extension!* Concentrate on full extension. Concentrate on bringing the clubhead away and up so that it is as far away from your body as your arms will extend. And as the clubhead rises above your shoulders, concentrate on bringing your hands as high as possible, even if the shaft dips below parallel to the ground.

At the same time—and this is another reason for a very, very S-L-O-W upswing—take the time to make a full body turn or coil. You'll notice in the photo on page 22 that my knees, hips and shoulders are slowly making a full turn to the right so that at least 90 percent of my weight at the top of the backswing is on my right leg.

In fact, I have shifted so much of my weight onto my right side that I have gone up three or four inches on my left toe.

By now, I am sure, you are aware that I have committed two golf no-no's. One, I dipped the shaft below parallel, a move that will usually throw the golfer off balance as he or she brings down the club. And, two, I lifted my left heel, which should stay glued to the ground or rise no more than about an inch. Lifting the left heel too high on the backswing, all the golf books tell you, throws the body out of position on the downswing—and you get a mis-hit. And the golf books are right.

But by lifting the left heel and bringing the clubhead below parallel, I have increased the height and width of my swing path to maximum. If I bring down the club on the same path that I brought it up, the clubhead will travel through an arc that is the most extended I can make it. The wider the arc, the faster the clubhead speed at impact—which means I will really rocket that ball.

Unless, of course, my body falls from a straight to a tilted position during the downswing and the clubhead jumps out of its proper swing path. Then we have a mis-hit—and trouble.

And that's what will usually happen—the body falling out of its straight position—when you dip the clubhead below parallel and lift the left heel too high. Look at my position at the top of my upswing (see photo) and you can see that the club is below parallel and only the toe of my left foot is on the ground. Almost anything can happen as I bring down the club—and nearly all the things are bad.

However—and this is an important "however"—I have what I call "a friend" who will help to hold the club in its proper arc even if my body moves out of position during the downswing. That "friend" is the strength in my hands, wrists and forearms, gained from the Golf Connection exercises I give you for each day.

Nevertheless, even with the help of that "friend," I must have a solid foundation during the downswing. Therefore, just before I begin the downswing, I make a move that will ensure a solid foundation and bring my hands, knees, hips and shoulders all in proper synch for the downswing.

At the top of my upswing, I bring down that left heel—hard! I may even stamp down so hard with that left heel that I can hear it hit the ground. That stamping sound is my signal to start the downswing. I have made the highest and fullest backswing. Then—with the planting of the left heel—I have steadied my body for a downswing that will keep the club in the same arc that it traced during the upswing.

If the downswing now follows the path of the upswing, the clubhead will be moving at maximum speed as it comes closer to the impact zone. Tomorrow we'll learn how to bring down the club at max speed—and then how to turn max speed into super-max speed.

Drill for the Power Upswing

Stand at arm's length away from a wall that's on your right side. Simulate a takeaway swing, bringing the arms back as slowly and as straight as possible. Concentrate on keeping the arms straight and extended during the first two feet of the takeaway—and keep them straight and fully extended until your fingers brush the wall. At that level, just about waist level, the wrists will begin to cock and the arms begin to bend slightly so

Concentrate on keeping the arms straight until your fingers brush the wall.

25

that the hands come up *and over* the right ear. Do this for 15 to 30 minutes, concentrating on bringing up the extended arms slowly until you feel the fingertips brush the wall. That will be your signal to turn your shoulders so that the left shoulder comes under and touches your chin. The brushing of the fingertips will also be the signal for your arms to bend slightly as your hands come high and above the head.

Exercises for the Golf Connection

Buy a hand squeezer like the one I am holding (see photo). Made of coiled steel, these squeezers are terrific hand and arm strengtheners; you can squeeze them

Hand squeezers are terrific hand and arm strengtheners.

anywhere and anytime, even while you are taking a bath or a stroll. You can also squeeze a rubber ball. One of my favorite hand-squeezing exercises is to take a bath towel in one hand or in both hands and squeeze all that fluff into a tight ball.

If you like to lift weights, do curls with a weight no more than three pounds, lifting the weight toward you, then away from you. One of my favorite weight-lifting exercises will also impress on your muscle memory the right moves for the golf swing. Hold two three-pound weights, one in each hand. Simulate the upswing by lifting the weight in the right hand so that the weight rises above the shoulder while the left hand holds the weight in the same position that you would use for gripping a golf club. Then simulate the downswing by bringing the weight in the right hand down to the left hand. Then simulate the through swing by bringing the weight in the left hand up above the left shoulder. Do this for 15 to 30 minutes.

The Power Downswing

Let's go back to where we were just before the end of yesterday's lesson. You are holding the club at the top of your upswing. Your left heel is three or four inches off the ground, the clubhead is dipping below parallel.

Now you bring down that left heel—hard! You have begun what I call the forward move that will shift your weight, now about 90 percent on your back leg, toward your front leg. At impact, the weight will be about 90 percent on your front leg.

As I drop my left heel to cement my foundation and create a platform for my downswing, the clubhead drops to about shoulder height. I have begun to advance it toward the Impact Zone.

Now let's freeze the action for a moment. As I pointed out in *Break 100 in 21 Days*, a golf swing has lower-gear action—the movement of the feet, knees and hips—and upper-gear action, which is the movement of the arms, torso and shoulders.

Here's the action of the upper gear for the power downswing: The forward move continues with the arms unfolding to extend as straight as they were on

On the downswing, wrists are ahead of the clubhead as the clubhead comes to waist level, and arms are fully extended. The right heel is rising, knees and hips are turning toward the ball.

Keep the left arm straight on the downswing. The left arm must swing along the intended line of flight.

the upswing. My wrists are ahead of the clubhead as the clubhead comes down to about waist level. That's important: The wrists must stay ahead of the clubhead until we enter the Impact Zone.

While the upper gear brings down the club in a fully extended arc and the right shoulder drops so that it is again almost even with the left shoulder, my lower gear—hips, knees and feet—are making their forward move. They come around so that the right heel rises off the ground and the knees and hips turn toward the ball. As the clubhead comes to about waist level, at least 70 to 80 percent of my weight has now shifted to the front leg. I am close to completing what I call the "slingshot effect," which turns average-distance golfers into super-distance golfers.

Three important reminders during the downswing:

1. To prevent the tendency to hook the ball with that strong grip, I advise power golfers to keep the left arm straight as it comes down. The left arm must swing on a path that is the intended line of flight. Remember: The straight left arm on the downswing is the rod that connects the action of the upper and lower gears.

2. Keep the head, as it was at address, behind the ball. If the head stays behind the ball during the downswing, you are helping to ensure that the clubhead is tracing the same extended arc or path on the downswing that it traced on the upswing. In short, you are helping to make sure that the clubhead impacts the ball and not the ground behind the ball.

3. Keep the shoulders parallel to the target line as the right shoulder drops. If the shoulders turn left or

Keep the shoulders parallel to the target line, the line indicated here by the club in my left hand.

If the shoulders turn away from the target line, as mine are turning here, the ball will go away from the target.

right, you are going to swing the clubhead in the direction the shoulders are moving. The ball will go to the left or to the right of the target line.

How fast should you bring down the clubhead? My answer: As fast as you can bring it down while keeping all the units of the upper and lower gears in synch. If you brought the club up at 35 miles an hour, bring it down at 40 miles an hour. If your shots are going wide of the target, slow the downswing and bring the club down at 30 miles an hour. As your accuracy increases, step on the gas. Try to increase the speed to 40 or 45 miles an hour. If you can get it to 50 miles an hour—about 50 percent faster than you took up the club—you will be entering the Impact Zone with max clubhead speed.

Tomorrow we will see how to juice up that speed to super max.

Drills for the Downswing

1. Stand at arm's length from a wall on your right side. Using only your hands and arms, assume the position at the top of the backswing: left heel high off the ground, the hands held high and the wrists cocked so the clubhead would be below parallel if you were holding a club. Bring down your hands and arms so your fingertips just graze the wall. As your fingertips go by the wall, check to make sure that your wrists are in front of your hands. Do this for about a half hour, bringing down your arms and hands very slowly at first, but gradually increasing the speed while making sure that your fingers brush the wall and your wrists stay in front of your hands.

As you bring down your hands and your fingertips brush the wall, make sure that the wrists are in front of your hands.

2. Holding a club, stand a club's length away from a rope stretched between two posts and about waist high. From the top of your upswing, bring down the club so that the head catches the rope. As the clubhead catches the rope on the downswing, check to make sure that your wrists are ahead of the clubhead. Do this slowly at first, then pick up your speed so that the clubhead catches the rope with the wrists ahead of the clubhead.

3. Hold a club against your chest with your left hand so that it is parallel to the ground. Using only your right hand, simulate an upswing and a downswing. Make sure that the clubhead is always pointing along

When the club catches the waist-high rope, the wrists should be ahead of the clubhead.

the line of flight, not to the left (meaning you closed your shoulders) or to the right (meaning you opened your shoulders).

Exercises for the Golf Connection

Swinging weighted clubs is an excellent way to build strength in the wrists and forearms while also grooving your golf swing. And you can swing clubs almost any-

Simulate the coiling action of the golf swing by first turning so the left elbow and left knee point at the ball, then turning so the right elbow and right knee point at the ball.

where. You can also swing two clubs at once. Or you can buy weights that are easily attached to clubs. I like to swing my sand wedge for a few minutes each day, since the sand wedge is the heaviest club in a golfer's bag. Swing a sand wedge, two clubs together or weighted clubs for 15 minutes.

Here's an exercise to strengthen back and leg muscles while also impressing on your muscle memory the coiling action of the body that you need for a full body turn. Take a golf stance, the ball placed midway in your stance. Put both hands on your hips and simulate a takeaway turn so that the left elbow and left knee are pointing at the ball. Then make a full turn so that the right elbow and right knee are pointing at the ball. Do this for 15 minutes.

The Late, Late Power Release

All golfers, especially those averaging around 100, know that you put zing into your shots with the so-called "late release"—the releasing, or uncocking, of the wrists just before impact.

But when I teach late release to golfers who want to hit for more distance, I say this: "What we are looking for is the best time to release. We don't want to time our release during the first moments of the downswing; you are imparting max speed to your clubhead—but at the wrong time. The clubhead is nowhere near the impact area—and that's where the ball is sitting. It's the ball we want to strike—not empty air."

So you want to release the wrists at the most effective moment in the swing. What's the most effective moment? Here's how I teach golfers how to find the right moment in their swing for them to release their wrists and apply the extra energy that adds zip to clubhead speed:

I stand to one side as the golfer brings down the clubhead. As the clubhead comes even with the golfer's waist, I hold the clubhead so that the golfer must apply

As the clubhead comes even with the golfer's waist, I grip the clubhead, teaching the golfer when to uncock the wrists for the late release.

extra force to continue bringing the clubhead down. He gets that extra force by (1) speeding up the downward swing, and (2) uncocking the wrists.

That's what he should do in a real power swing. As the clubhead comes down past the right hip, speed up the swing, then uncock the wrists.

I explain that to the golfer this way: "I grabbed the clubhead at about waist level. The clubhead was entering the lower quadrant of your swing arc. And it's somewhere in that lower quadrant where you should release the wrists."

What we are talking about, in short, is not a *late release*, but a release at some point in the lower quadrant of the swing arc that will make the release the most effective release *for you*.

We are all built differently. We all have different arm, wrist and hand strength. We are all different in our ability to coordinate all the elements in a swing.

I can release my wrists a few inches from the ball and make solid contact with my club's sweet spot. Fred Couples can release his wrists, I am sure, even closer to the ball than I can. As a result, Fred Couples gets the late release and impacts the ball with more clubhead velocity than I can generate. His clubhead is traveling at top speed at impact, while mine has lost some velocity because it must travel a slightly longer distance.

Now, what does this mean to you and your hopes of timing your release so that you boom that ball out there 10 to 20 or 30 more yards?

First of all, you will have stronger wrists and forearms than you did when we began, because you have been doing your daily Golf Connection exercises. The stronger your Golf Connection—the hands, wrists and arms—the more force and speed you can apply to the working part of your tool, and that's the clubhead.

But I must be realistic with you: Some of you will always release a longer distance from impact than someone who plays as often as I do. Put another way, your release may be late but other golfers will release even later. And that's because, as I explained, some of us can do things that other people can't do. Some of us can swing a club at, say, 60 miles an hour and impact the ball with the club's sweet spot. Others can't swing that fast and still impact the ball with the sweet spot.

Now let me show you how to release your wrists at the

41

distance from the ball that's right for your skill and strength.

As we discussed yesterday, you are bringing down the clubhead with as much force and speed as you can muster while keeping your body straight. Your weight has shifted so that at least 90 percent has moved to your left side. Your right heel comes off the ground. The right shoulder—this is important—drops below the left shoulder. The clubhead is level with your waist.

Your clubhead has now entered the Release Zone, which is anywhere in the lower quadrant of your swing arc. Now—at any point in this lower quadrant—is the time to uncock your wrists by straightening them. Now is the time to pull the trigger and add that burst of speed to the clubhead. Now, in short, is the time to fire.

Golfers ask me: "But exactly at what point in the lower quadrant do I straighten my wrists?"

My answer: "The exact point at which you should release the wrists can't be pinpointed at two feet from the ball or two inches from the ball for all golfers. It could be two feet from the ball for a fast swinger; it could be two inches from the ball for a slow swinger. It could be 15 inches from the ball for a tall man with powerful wrists; it could be 20 inches from the ball for someone not built as powerfully.

"But this can be said with certainty: *For all golfers— big or small, athletically gifted or not—the wrist release must come in the Release Zone. And that zone is anywhere from when the clubhead has passed the waist to impact.*

Now let me give you what I call "the key to late-release power"—the right-shoulder signal.

At the top of your backswing, the right shoulder is above the left shoulder. As you bring down the clubhead, the right shoulder comes even with the left

The Release Zone is anywhere in the lower quadrant—that is, from when the clubhead has passed the waist to impact.

When the right shoulder drops below the left shoulder, that is your signal that you have entered the Release Zone.

Just before impact the wrists must straighten, as mine are here just after impact.

shoulder—as it was at address. As the clubhead comes lower, the right shoulder drops below the left shoulder.

When the right shoulder drops below the left, that is your signal that you have entered the Release Zone.

I know that you can't see the right shoulder drop below the left—your eyes are on the ball. But practice your downswing in slow motion as you watch it in a mirror. Straighten your wrists as the right shoulder comes below the left. You will be impressing on your muscle memory the timing of your late release.

As you build arm, wrist and hand strength and as you practice straightening the wrists exactly as you enter the Release Zone, you will be releasing closer and closer to the ball. After our fifteenth day together, you will be releasing the wrists at a point that is the right release point for you. It will be your own personal "late release."

Drills for Timing the Late, Late Release

1. Ask a friend to stand behind you as you bring down the clubhead slowly. As the clubhead comes to waist level, your friend should grip the clubhead lightly so that you feel resistance as you continue to bring down the club. Add force to the swing and snap the wrists so that the clubhead comes free of your friend's light hold. Practice this for about a half hour to impress on your muscle memory that the wrists must straighten somewhere during the lower quadrant of the swing arc.

2. To test whether or not you are releasing the wrists in the lower quadrant, take an iron and grip it by the neck with your left hand so that the butt is pointing to an imaginary ball on the ground.

Gripping a club by its neck, swing the shaft at an imaginary ball. The swishing sound should come from your left-leg side.

Swing at the ball with only your left hand so that the butt passes over the ball. You will hear a swishing sound as you release your wrist on the downswing. You want to hear that swishing sound coming from your left-leg side. That means you released the wrists before impact. If you hear the swishing sound on your right-leg side, you released your wrists too early.

Exercises for the Golf Connection

To strengthen the forearms and wrists enough to allow you to straighten your wrists late in the lower quadrant of the swing arc, repeat the two exercises for Day One: For a total of 30 minutes, "lift" a table or a desk with your fingertips; for another 30 minutes raise and lower your fists with your wrists resting on the arms of a chair. And, for another 30 minutes, squeeze a bath towel, 15 minutes with one hand, 15 minutes with the other.

The Power Impact and Follow-Through

Let's review our swing up to now:

We take a narrower stance, with the feet inside the shoulder line. We take a strong grip, with the left hand turned more to the right side.

We take a slower than normal backswing, with the arms fully extended away from the target; the weight shifts onto the right side, the left heel rises three or four inches.

We drop the left heel and begin the downswing; the wrists stay ahead of the clubhead; the club comes down at about twice the speed with which we brought the club up. And we keep the left arm swinging along the intended line of flight.

After we enter the Release Zone—that is, when the clubhead has passed the waist—we uncock, or straighten, the wrists for that snap-the-wrists action that adds zing and distance to the shot. It is much like the action you get when you snap a whip. As you bring the whip hand forward, the whip gets in front of the hand—just as the shaft and the clubhead get ahead of the hands after the wrists are released in the golf swing.

As the clubhead moves through the Impact Zone . . .

. . . the clubhead moves ahead of the wrists.

Now the clubhead enters the Impact Zone—that point in the swing's arc when the arms must be as straight as they were at address. The clubhead impacts the ball as squarely as the club was positioned at address. Then, as the clubhead moves through the Impact Zone, the clubhead moves ahead of the wrists.

It's what happens next that separates a power-hitting golfer from a golfer who hits for only average distance.

Average hitters impact the ball and think: "Great! I've done it! I hit the ball." And in effect, they quit on the swing. They neglect the fully extended follow-through.

Watch the long hitters. They go through the Impact Zone with the arms fully extended. The straight left arm is still a connecting rod, connecting the ball's flight to the ball's target. The left arm keeps straight along the line of flight. It doesn't come around and cross the line of flight, which would produce a roundhouse kind of baseball swing.

And the long hitters don't quit, even as their hands come up to the "shaking hands" position. Instead, their hands continue to come *up*—not around—with both arms straight until the clubhead reaches about eye level. Only then do their arms start to fold as the hands keep coming all the way up above the ears; the body now turns so that the feet, knees and belt buckle are facing the target.

Only then have the long hitters finished the swing.

Remember these key points for impact and follow-through in the power swing:

1. Come through the ball with more speed and force than you are used to. Instead of the golf club leading the way, your body leads. When the body leads, how-

Go through the Impact Zone to the "shaking hands" position with the arms fully extended.

Hands continue up above the ears; the body turns so that the feet, knees and belt buckle face the target.

ever, there is a possible pitfall. The body's momentum can cause you to finish with a baseball follow-through: the clubhead below the shoulders. Don't let this happen! We want the hands, arms, and clubhead to finish above the shoulders.

2. To avoid hooking, your left arm must be straight at impact, as it clears the left side of your body, almost to the point where your hands are above your shoulders. Just as you would release a bowling ball and continue to raise your arm (so that the ball goes straight), continue to raise your arms even after you have struck the golf ball. You are encouraging the arms and hands to keep on a straight line (so that you don't impact the ball with a glancing blow that causes hooks or slices).

3. Make a conscious effort to extend your arms in the follow-through.

4. Your weight should come around so that you finish with a full body turn, only the toe of your right foot on the ground (not the heel) and the center of your body facing the target.

Drills for Impact and Follow-Through

We want to encourage the left arm to be dominant and finish above the shoulders. (If you are a left-hander, the reverse is true.) Since most of us are right-handed, when we get tired the right hand has a tendency to take over for the left. When that happens, we are likely to let the left arm cross over the intended line of flight, causing a hook or a slice. Hold the club by the neck and swing only with the left hand, swinging in slow motion and concentrating on keeping your left arm straight

Just as you continue to raise your arm after releasing a bowling ball, continue to raise your arms after striking a golf ball. The left arm should not cross the intended line of flight, producing a baseball swing.

from impact until the butt end of the club passes your shoulders and your right shoulder touches your chin. Do this for a half hour to an hour, impressing on your muscle memory the need to keep that connecting rod straight from impact to the "shaking hands" position of the follow-through.

Exercises for the Golf Connection

Squeeze your hand squeezer for a total of a half hour. Sit in a chair and extend your hands and wrists, lifting the balled fists up and down for a total of a half hour.

DAY SIX

The Lower-Gear Action for Super Power

Let's suppose you are about to play a long par-4, this one about 440 yards.

With your new power swing, you can reach the green in three shots with a 220-yard tee shot, a 180-yard iron shot, then a short pitch. But you have often dreamed about getting to this green in two.

This has been an excellent round for you so far. You are feeling good about your swing. This tee is elevated, and the fairway slopes downhill and yawns wide. Today a strong wind is blowing toward the green.

Let's go for our par!

I'll show you how. I call it shifting down from *the upper gear* to *the lower gear*. You're going to use the same power swing we've been working on since Day One. But just as you shift down to get more power when you drive a car up a steep hill, you can also shift down to get more power when you want extra distance in golf.

Of course, the driver of a car downshifts only when

the car needs extra power. I tell weekend golfers: "Only shift down—at the most—four or five times during a round. True, the lower-gear action can get you more distance, but, one, it can also cause you to mis-hit and land in trouble. Two, shifting to lower-gear action—the action used by the touring pros—is tricky in its timing; thus it's almost impossible to repeat the swing with consistency during an entire round. That's why you're a weekend golfer and Fred Couples is a millionaire touring pro. Third, as we'll see in our lesson on course management, getting extra distance is not always the wisest strategy.

Let's get straight what I mean by lower gear and upper gear. The upper gear is the shoulders, torso, arms, wrists and hands. The lower gear is the hips, legs, knees and feet. Connecting the upper gear with the lower gear is what I call the *connecting rod*—the straight left arm at impact. If the left arm is bent or bowed at impact, as I pointed out in *Break 100 in 21 Days*, the upper gear's power cannot connect with the lower gear's power.

All amateur golfers, even low-handicappers, use upper-gear action. As they bring down the clubhead to about waist level—the beginning of the Release Zone— they shift their weight so that they are evenly balanced: 50 percent of their weight on the front leg, 50 percent on the back leg. Then, as the clubhead comes closer to impact, the clubhead's speed and force bring most of the rest of the weight forward onto the front foot. That's upper-gear action.

The touring pros use lower-gear action. I demonstrate lower-gear action in the photos that follow.

I bring up the club as I would for upper-gear action. When my left shoulder touches my chin, the upswing has been completed. Now I bring down the club at about twice the speed that I brought up the club.

Up to now, nothing has changed. We have not yet shifted down to lower-gear action. But as the clubhead comes to about waist level—as I enter the Release Zone—my hips and knees make an abrupt and rapid shift to the left. I have moved most of my weight onto my left leg. I am out of balance.

That is the key to lower-gear action. With upper-gear action I would be in balance—my weight evenly distributed on both legs—as I bring the clubhead down through the Release Zone.

But now, as I release my wrists and fire the clubhead just before impact, most of my weight is on my front leg. And just like a boxer who throws a punch with most of his weight on the front foot, I throw the clubhead at the ball with much more force and clubhead speed than if my weight were evenly balanced.

With upper-gear action, the clubhead leads the parade, bringing the body around to face the target. It also brings the arms and hands up above the shoulders to a high and full follow-through.

But with lower-gear action, the left hip leads as the clubhead comes through the Impact Zone.

After impact, however, we want the clubhead—not the left hip—to lead for a high and full follow-through.

Why? Because if the left hip continues to lead, it will turn the body around—the same way a baseball batter's body turns when he swings at a pitch. The clubhead will cross the intended line of flight—and we hook or slice.

We want the clubhead to catch up with the left hip and lead us into the follow-through. And the clubhead does catch up because it is now traveling at a much

Keys to lower-gear action: On the upswing, make sure the shoulder turn completes itself and your weight is mostly on the right leg.

On the downswing, the weight shifts quickly to the left leg.

As the clubhead passes between the waist and right knee, it's somewhere in that zone that the straightening of the wrists should begin.

The clubhead catches up with the left hip after impact. Your arms fold after they pass the belt buckle. Finish with your hands high.

faster speed than the left hip, which has already made its move. The left hip is now turning toward the target—but at a snail's pace.

The clubhead passes the hip and clears the left side of the body. The clubhead leads the body, shoulders, arms and wrists into a full and high follow-through, with the hands finishing above the shoulders and the body facing the target.

One danger in shifting down: Your subconscious mind—or your muscle memory—may try to block the early weight shift to the front. "This is not the way you always swing," the muscle memory may tell you. A momentary hesitation on the downswing, I don't have to tell you, can lead to lots of things, all bad.

Before you swing, therefore, remind your subconscious that you are going to shift the weight early to the front leg. The subconscious should be warned not to block the early movement of the knees and hips to the left. Take several practice swings to remind your muscle memory that this is a move you want to make.

True, you will hit some bad shots with lower-gear action. This is not the controlled swing of upper-gear action. Shift down, as I said, only when you feel your timing is right, the strategy is right and trouble areas are few and far between.

But the plus side, as I tell golfers, is this: "With upper-gear action, you are *swinging at* a golf ball. With lower-gear action, you are *hitting* a golf ball.

Drill for Upper- and Lower-Gear Action

Stand two or three inches from a door on your left that can swing away from you, but not toward you. Simulate a swing with your hands so that first your fingertips

If your left hip continues to lead, it will turn the body around and the clubhead will cross the intended line of flight.

Pushing open the door with your fingertips simulates the weight shift for upper-gear action.

Pushing open the door with your left hip simulates the weight shift for lower-gear action.

brush the door on the follow-through, and then the left hip touches the door. Shift your weight properly for upper-gear action. Your weight should be evenly balanced just before or at impact, with most of the weight shifting to the front side after impact. Do this for 15 to 30 minutes.

Again, simulate a swing with your hands. As the hands pass your right hip, move your knees and hips to the left so that first the left hip brushes against the door, then the fingertips brush the door. That's the proper weight shift for lower-gear action. You should be out of balance just before impact. Practice this drill for 15 to 30 minutes each day until, at a driving range, you can use lower-gear action to hit 10 straight balls without a mis-hit.

Exercises for the Golf Connection

Repeat the lifting-the-table isometric exercise for Day One. Squeeze your hand squeezer for at least a total of 30 minutes during the day.

DAY SEVEN

The Power Swing With Fairway Woods

So far I have discussed using the power swing off the tee with a driver. Let me add that the power swing is the same swing for all the clubs. You can't change swings as you change clubs. Learning one swing is tough enough.

But you must keep certain keys in mind as you move off the tee to the fairway. When you swing at the ball off the tee, the ball is teed up and essentially it is already in the air. So, when you swing at a ball on the fairway, your first job is to get the ball up into the air. To do that, bring down the club in a descending arc, not with the sweeping arc you would use to sweep a ball off a tee.

During the next five days, I am going to give you keys to keep in mind for successful power shots with different clubs from different lies.

With the fairway woods, there is less margin for error in the Impact Zone than there is for a tee shot. That's because the ball on a tee offers a bigger target: from the ball's equator to its bottom. A ball on the fairway presents a much smaller target, since we must aim to contact the ball at its bottom. If we hit the ball at the equator when the ball is sunk in grass, we'll top or "skull" the shot. We must contact the bottom of the ball with the clubhead to get the ball up. So the margin for error shrinks when we move off the tee to swing at balls on the fairway with woods or irons.

Let's look at the power swing with a fairway wood. Stand at address with the clubhead square to the bottom of the ball. The clubhead is connected to the club's straight shaft. The shaft is connected to your lower gear and upper gear by a straight left arm.

It is imperative on all shots, but especially on fairway-wood shots, that the left arm—the connecting rod—stay straight at impact. If the left arm bends or bows, you will not impact the ball at its bottom. Instead, you will hit the ball at or above the equator, and you'll probably hit it with a glancing blow. Result: a slice, a hook or a topped shot.

When we take the club to the top of the backswing, we will, of necessity, bend the left arm. But as we start the downswing, the left arm must become what we call "responsive." It must respond to the power swing's speed by straightening quickly as the swift-moving clubhead comes to waist level—the start of the Release Zone.

The left arm must stay straight as the clubhead is released and enters the Impact Zone. The left arm must be as straight at impact as it was at address. But it must not be so stiff and hard that the swing loses its flow. With the fairway woods we want to achieve a flowing swing that will sweep the ball off the grass.

After impact, the left arm must continue to respond to the power swing's speed by keeping straight for the first half of the follow-through. Only after the clubhead rises above waist level—the "shaking hands" position—does the left arm (and the right arm) begin to fold.

The left arm must be as straight at impact as it was at address.

After impact the left arm must stay straight until the clubhead rises above waist level. The left arm is now the rod that connects the ball's flight to the target.

To sum up, when swinging for power with the fairway woods, your key thought should be: Straight left arm at release, through impact and into the first half of the follow-through.

Drill for the Power Swing With the Fairway Woods

Grip a club by the neck with your left hand. Using only the left arm, bring back the club to the top of the backswing. Bring down the club and swing it through an imaginary ball, continuing into the follow-through. You should hear a swish coming from below you as the butt end of the club passes over the imaginary ball. If you hear a swish, your left arm was straight at impact; it was responsive. If you don't hear a swish, your left arm was probably bent.

To make sure that you are getting left-arm response, make this a regular drill before you go onto a course or a driving range.

Exercises for the Golf Connection

Repeat the exercises for Day Five.

The Power Swing
With Long Irons

The daily Golf Connection exercises will have added strength in your fingers, hands and wrists, but you are not likely to have the strong hands and wrists you need to swing the number one-iron properly. I would recommend carrying in your bag the two-, three- and four-irons, or at least two of those three.

Keeping the left arm straight at impact is as important with the long irons as it is with the fairway woods. But we do have a margin for error when swinging with the fairway woods that we don't have when we swing the long irons.

Let me explain why:

We sweep the ball off the grass with the fairway woods, much as we sweep the ball off the tee with the driver. The loft of the fairway woods gets the ball up.

But with the long irons, we impact the ball with a descending blow rather than with a sweeping blow. By striking the ball while the swing is still in its descending arc, the loft of the iron's clubface impels the ball upward. Remember: With irons you hit down. You impact the ball first, then grass.

Now here's why you have less margin for error at

75

impact with the long irons than with the fairway woods: If you impact the ball with the fairway woods anywhere below the equator, you will hit a reasonably successful shot. If you impact the ball with the irons anywhere except at the bottom of the ball, you get a "skulled" shot that starts out fast and drops short.

Therefore, the two keys to a successful power swing with the long irons are:

One, make sure the left arm is responding quickly by straightening as the clubhead enters the Release Zone. It must stay straight at impact so that it contacts the ball at the same spot it contacted the ball at address. The left arm must stay straight as the clubhead comes up into the follow-through. The left arm must be swinging down the intended line of flight, pointing toward the target. If you let the left arm cross the line of flight to your left, you will hook. If you let the left arm cross the line of flight to your right, you will slice. The left arm is still the connecting rod. But now—this is important—it is also the rod connecting the flight of the ball to its target.

Second, you must keep your head in the same position at impact that it was in at address. If you faced the ball at address, face the ball at impact. If you faced a spot just behind the ball at address, face that same spot at impact.

Golfers have a tendency, when trying to get extra distance with these long irons, to fall slightly back to "scoop" the ball and get it airborne quickly. Or they tend to push forward to add "oomph" and get more distance. They try to use their bodies to do the job instead of allowing the clubhead to do the job it was designed to do.

When they lean back or move forward, they change

Keep your head, at impact, in the same position it was in at address.

Leaning back or moving forward to "scoop" the ball into the air will change the landing area of the clubhead.

Simulating a swing with your arms and hands, keep your eyes on the same spot on the ground until the right shoulder touches your chin and brings your head around.

the landing area of the clubhead. Most likely, they hit behind the ball—hitting "fat," as we say—which means a droopy shot.

Also, if you pitch backward or forward with your body, you will change the angle, or loft, of the clubface as it comes to impact. You will open or close the clubface. If you open it, you slice. If you close it, you hook.

I hear golfers tell one another: "You lifted your head." That's bad, but moving the head to the left or right is just as bad, especially with these long irons, which have relatively straight clubfaces. A slight change in the angle of your head to the ball can mean a big change in the angle of the clubface to the ball.

Here's a simple key for keeping your head at the same angle to the ball from address to after impact: Keep your head steady until your right shoulder comes up, touches the chin and moves your head to the left. Nothing else should move it.

Drill for the Power Swing With the Long Irons

Using only your arms and hands, make a simulated takeaway swing. When your left shoulder touches your chin and you then bring down your arms and hands, keep your eyes on the same spot on the ground until your right shoulder touches your chin and brings your head around. Do this for a half hour. Also use this drill as a practice swing on the course before you swing with one of the long irons.

Exercises for the Golf Connection

Do the two exercises you did on Day Five for a total of an hour.

The Power Swing
With Medium Irons

Most golfers feel best when they are swinging with the five-, six- and seven-irons. They feel comfortable because the shafts are a manageable length and do not place them too far away from the ball; and they are not so short that they feel they are crouching too low or standing too close to the ball.

What's more, with the medium irons you are more confident because you know that even if you move your head or your body a little bit and mis-hit the ball, the loft of the clubhead will get the ball up and toward your target. You may not land close to the pin, but if you land on the green 40 feet from the pin, you are satisfied.

What this means to the power swing: Since these clubs are more forgiving, you can swing more aggressively. Instead of coming down at 50 miles an hour, as you might with the longer irons, you can come down at 60 miles an hour.

If you have been getting 120 to 130 yards with a six-iron, say, with a more aggressive swing you can get up to 140 yards. That can make the difference between being short of the green and needing three strokes to hole out, instead of being on the green and needing only one or two strokes to hole out.

Let's go to the power swing with a medium iron. Bring the club back to parallel or even below parallel—just as you do with the longer clubs. Never shorten your backswing, even with the short irons, unless you want to do something different, such as a punch shot between trees or a pitch-and-roll. You should always take your club back above the shoulders—to the high zone—because that helps to ensure that you will strike the ball with a downward blow, enabling the clubhead to get the ball up.

Bring down the club faster than with the longer irons. As you pass the Release Zone—clubhead passing the right hip—the club's shorter shaft will produce a shorter radius in the arc of the swing than with a longer iron.

What this means to you:

The clubhead will get to the ball sooner and quicker than with a longer club (since the clubhead has a shorter distance to travel to the Impact Zone). The shorter radius of the swing arc means your wrists must release sooner. Put another way, because of the shorter shaft and shorter arc, there is much less lag time from when the clubhead passes the waist until it impacts the ball.

Therefore, hand-and-wrist action—the release of the clubhead—must happen much more quickly because of that shorter arc between the Release Zone and the Impact Zone.

This may seem strange to the subconscious—wrists and hands responding quicker and sooner than with the longer clubs. The subconscious may try to slow

The clubhead of a medium iron, like the one in my right hand, will get to the ball faster than the clubhead of a wood, like the one in my left hand, because the swing arc of the medium iron is shorter. Thus your wrists must release more quickly than with the longer clubs.

down or stop the action, thinking this is all happening too soon.

Don't let that happen. As you practice with the medium irons, tell your subconscious that this is what you want to do—release the wrists quicker and impact the ball quicker than with longer-shafted clubs.

But it's after impact when most golfers make their big mistake with the medium irons—a mistake that is fatal to a power swing. They quit. There is no high and full follow-through.

Here's why they make that mistake: Because impact has come sooner and quicker than with the longer-shafted clubs, golfers get a scary notion as they feel the clubhead impact the ball. They fear the ball may go too far—and they stop the follow-through.

They hit and stop. They don't make a full and high follow-through. They punch at the ball. They lose distance as the ball drops short. And because the left hand or the right hand is likely to cross the line of flight after they quit on the shot, the ball goes left or right of the target.

Remember: Once you impact, that's only the first half of your job as a power swinger. The second half of the job is to finish on the other side of the swing with a high and above-the-shoulders follow-through that will get you both distance and accuracy.

So there are two keys to the power swing with the medium irons:

1. The wrists must respond quicker than with the longer-shafted clubs by straightening just after they enter the Release Zone (because the clubhead has a shorter distance to travel from Release Zone to Impact Zone).

2. The through part of the swing must be as extended and as high as the swing with the longer-shafted clubs.

Drills for the Power Swing With the Medium Irons

1. Take a medium iron by the neck with your left hand and bring it back so that the shaft is parallel to the ground. Bring the shaft down and through, finishing with the shaft above your shoulders and pointing away from your target. Make sure you hear the swishing sound *after* the shaft has passed your right leg, but make sure you continue the swing until the shaft is high and above your shoulders, just as though you were swinging a longer club. Do that for 15 to 30 minutes.

2. Take a fairway wood and make a practice swing at an imaginary ball. Finish with the clubhead high and above your shoulders. Hold yourself in that position for a few seconds, as though you were posing for a photograph. Then immediately take a medium iron, make the same swing at an imaginary ball and again make the same over-the-shoulder and full-extension follow-through that you just did with the fairway wood. Get that feeling of the full, over-the-shoulder finish that you felt with the fairway wood. Keep doing that, one swing with the fairway wood, one swing with the medium iron, for 15 to 30 minutes.

Exercises for the Golf Connection

Repeat the exercises for Day Six for a total of 30 minutes.

Alternate swinging with a fairway wood and a medium iron to get the feeling of a full finish with the medium irons.

The Power Swing With Short Irons

Watch most weekend golfers. When it comes to the forcefulness of their swing, they have their thinking backwards.

When they face a long shot of, say, 220 yards, they swing a driver or a fairway wood with all the power they can muster. They swing at a hundred or so miles an hour, forgetting that they are swinging a club that is built to get them that distance.

Now watch when they take a short iron and face a shot of, say, 80 yards. They take a swing that is slow enough to get them a traffic ticket for driving too slowly on a super highway—say, at 20 miles an hour.

But the reverse should be true: Swing easy with the long clubs; swing forcefully with the short clubs.

I am sure you understand why. The driver is a rifle built for distance with its very long shaft, its big head and its straight clubface. So we want to swing slow enough to make sure we take advantage of that long shaft by making a wide swing arc, which will build clubhead speed.

But when we grip a short iron to hit to a green less than a hundred yards away, we are holding a popgun. Since the shaft is the shortest of all the clubs, the radius of the swing arc will be shorter than with the other clubs. Therefore, the clubhead speed will be slower at impact than if we had swung a longer iron with the same arm and hand action.

Result: We need more forceful arm and hand action with the shorter clubs—to boost clubhead speed— than with the longer clubs.

And there is another reason for swinging the short irons faster than the longer clubs. With the short irons we dig into the turf—we take a divot—more deeply than we do with the medium irons. The short irons are built to dig deeply into the turf after impact, creating the backspin that makes the ball stop quickly so it does not roll off the putting surface.

If clubhead speed does not accelerate before impact when we are swinging a short iron, the turf is likely to slow down or even stop the clubhead. The follow-through will not be full and high, the hands perhaps going no higher than the waist. The ball will land short, and if the hands cross the line of flight, it will land left or right of the target.

The important thing to remember with the short irons, then, is to come down with the club much more aggressively than with the medium or long irons.

The short irons are the clubs we use for accuracy. We shoot for the fairway with the long irons; we shoot for the green with the medium irons; we shoot for the pin with the short irons.

The short irons are built with wide heads and lofted faces to get the ball high into the air and then stop it quickly on the putting surface. If you don't meet the ball with the sweet spot, their lofted faces are very forgiving.

So you can swing faster with a short iron, trusting the clubface to do the job, which is to get the ball high into the air and to go whatever distance the club was built to cover. You can swing more aggressively and not be as likely to be penalized for a mis-hit as you would be for a mis-hit with a long iron.

Finally, we must swing more aggressively with the short irons than with any other club because of their short shafts; the short shaft of a nine-iron will not trace as wide an arc as the longer shaft of a four-iron. Since the arc of a nine-iron is not as wide as the arc of a longer-shafted club, the clubhead speed is slower. We must boost the clubhead speed by swinging not at 40 miles an hour but at 50 or more miles per hour.

And since the arc is not as wide as the arc of a longer iron, the clubhead will travel even more quickly than the medium or long irons from release to impact. That means we must release the wrists even faster than we do for the medium irons.

That's the first half of the power swing with the short irons: a full backswing, an aggressive downswing, quick release of the wrists, impact the ball and then contact the turf with a descending blow.

But that's only the first half. Too many golfers slow down the swing after impacting the turf. Sometimes the turf makes them slow down or even stop. Or they may think: "Gee, I've hit the ball too hard. It's going to go over the green."

What happens next, of course, is predictable. There is no follow-through, so the shot lacks oomph and drops short of the green (where, more often than not, there are more bunkers than in back of the green). Even worse, the wimpish follow-through—no straight left arm acting as a connecting rod between the ball and the target—causes the left arm to cross over the target line and the ball goes to the right. Or the right arm crosses the target line and the ball goes to the left.

With the longer clubs, the power swing gives you distance. With the shorter clubs, such as the eight-iron, nine-iron and the pitching wedge, the power swing gives you accuracy. Here are the keys to power-swing accuracy with the short irons:

1. Take a full upswing to build leverage and momentum, with your hands rising above the shoulders and the clubhead about parallel with the ground or just short of parallel. A descending blow is especially important with the short irons—since we want to take a deeper divot—and a full upswing will help to create a steeply descending downswing.

2. Grip the club a little more firmly with the fingers than you would with a longer club. Don't choke it, but a firm grip is necessary because you will be cutting deeper into the turf than with the other irons, and you must keep the clubhead square to the target line.

3. Allow the short irons, with their deep heads and sharply angled faces, to cut into the turf after impacting the ball. That will give you the height and backspin the club was designed to produce. You don't want to

pick the ball off the turf or sweep it off. Remember, hit down to get the ball up.

4. After impact, continue the swing, with your arms staying straight and pointing to the target until your hands are at the "shaking hands" position. Only then do the arms begin to fold.

5. Finish with your hands and clubhead high above your shoulders—as high above your shoulders as they were at the top of the upswing. This is important when swinging with any club, but it is especially important with the short irons because it helps to ensure accuracy. Match the ends!

Drill for the Power Swing With the Short Irons

Tack down a sheet of newspaper by placing four tees into the ground through the four corners of the paper. Aim at an imaginary ball placed in the center of the sheet of paper. Swing a short iron so that you contact the paper right behind the ball and then shear the paper to its end as you swing the club through the Impact Zone and up into a high and full follow-through. Do this 10 times, using a new sheet of paper for each swing. You are teaching your swing to enter turf and continue all the way through the turf to a full follow-through.

Exercises for the Golf Connection

Repeat the exercises for Day Six.

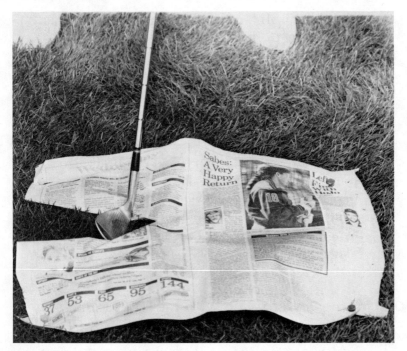

Shear the newspaper to its end.

DAY ELEVEN

Power Your Way Out of Trouble

For today's lesson, let me put you into three trouble areas on a golf course and show you how your new power swing can get you out.

TROUBLE NO. 1

This is a long par-4 hole or a par-5 hole. On either hole you want to gobble up as much distance as you can on each of your fairway shots. Depending on your handicap, and whether it is a par-4 or a par-5, you are aiming to reach the green in two, three or four shots.

Now let's assume that on the tee you made a mis-hit. In your eagerness to gobble up distance, you sliced the ball into the woods on the right side of the fairway.

Now, 90 percent of the time when you hit into rough or woods, the smartest thing you can do is accept the mis-hit and pitch the ball back onto the nearest part of the fairway—even if you have to give up distance and go backward. Looking for miracle shots to get you out of trouble will only sink you into more trouble.

But, ah! There's good news today. You find your ball sitting on top of the rough. And while you are surrounded by low-hanging branches, you see there is an opening between the trees to the green. In short, this is a perfect situation to use the power swing to get out of trouble and grab as much distance as possible.

Here are two keys to remember when you hit out of rough and between trees:

1. You need lower-gear action with quicker-than-usual hand-and-wrist action to make sure that the clubhead has enough force and speed to get through the rough and give you the distance.

2. You do not follow through as you usually do, with the hands above the shoulders. You stop the swing with the hands at about eye level.

Let's go through the mechanics of what is called the punch shot:

Make sure your hands grip the club extra firmly (because the rough will try to twist the clubhead). Take the club away with a full turn of the shoulders; the clubhead comes parallel or almost parallel to the ground. You need the full coiling and the full leverage of the backswing for that extra clubhead speed to whack the ball out of the rough.

As you start down with the club at about twice the speed you took it up, lean to the left with your left hip, shifting your weight quickly off your right leg into your left leg. You have shifted down to the lower gear. Straighten your wrists as the clubhead passes your right hip. Come *down and through* into the Impact Zone

Straighten your wrists early, as the clubhead passes your right hip.

hard and forcefully. This must be a descending blow; you must hit down to get the ball up. Don't let the rough cause you to quit on the swing. Continue the swing with the hands rising to the "shaking hands" position.

95

Stop as the hands reach the "shaking hands" position.

Now stop. The hands do not rise to the normal height for the full follow-through, with the clubhead above your shoulders. If you bring up your hands any higher, the ball will rise too quickly—maybe catching those low-hanging branches. You want a low line-drive trajectory for the ideal punch shot. But you will get accuracy because you kept your left arm straight after impact and into the follow-through. It is still acting as the connecting rod between the ball and the target.

TROUBLE NO. 2

You have hit into a fairway bunker. If the ball is sunk into the sand and there is a high bank or lip between you and the fairway, take the safest way out. Pitch the ball in a direction away from the green if you must, but get it onto the nearest fairway.

Most of the time, however, a ball will roll or bounce into a fairway bunker. It will usually be sitting on top of the sand. And many fairway bunkers have low lips. You don't need a high trajectory to get the ball out.

If you have a good lie and there is no lip, go for distance. Here are your three keys for hitting out of fairway bunkers: (1) Take a stronger club than the club you would use on the fairway for this distance, (2) choke down on the club, and (3) shift to upper-gear action.

Take a stronger club—a five, say, instead of a six— because after you hit down on the ball, the clubhead's descending arc is going to carry it into the sand. You will be taking a sand divot instead of a turf divot; and since sand is softer than turf, the club will dig deeper into the sand. If the club goes lower, the ball will go higher; that will take distance from the shot. To make up for that lost distance, select a stronger club.

Choke down slightly on the grip because you are swinging from an unsteady surface. Your spikes can't grip the sand the way they grip turf. To make sure you keep your body steady and that you contact the ball

Choke down on the club to shorten the arc of the swing from a fairway bunker.

Use mostly your hands, arms and shoulders—upper-gear action—
when hitting from a fairway bunker.

with the club's sweet spot, choke down on the club to shorten the arc of the swing.

Swing with upper-gear action—using mostly the hands, arms and shoulders—again because you are swinging from a slippery surface. Lower-gear action might cause your feet to slide, throwing the clubhead out of its proper path.

TROUBLE NO. 3

You have hit into the rough within 150 yards of the green, which is elevated. Your power swing can give you both the height and the distance that you need.

The key here is to remind yourself that you must be aggressive with your downswing. You must impact the ball at maximum clubhead speed to get the clubhead through the resistance of the rough and to cover the distance to the green. You must definitely go to lower gear.

Pick the club that you would select for this distance for a fairway shot. Why? First of all, you will feel comfortable with it. And you must trust the lower gear's extra power to get the elevation and distance that you will need.

As you stand over the ball, concentrate on getting balanced—weight distributed evenly on both legs.

As you start your takeaway, your key thought is this: "I am in no hurry." Do not let the rough cause you to make a faster turn or a harder and uncontrolled takeaway. You certainly don't strike the ball on the takeaway. By taking your time to put the club in position above your shoulders, you are making sure that you shift your weight to your right side. When your left shoulder touches your chin, you are ready to make your move down and through. *Down and through.* You must impact the ball with a descending blow.

Come down about twice as fast as you brought the club up. As the club starts down, slide your left hip and knee to the left side, making that early weight shift that puts you out of balance. Your knees are now coming around in what I call the slingshot effect, created by the lower gear. Your wrists straighten as they rush to catch up with your left hip and pass it, boosting the club-head's speed at impact.

After impact your key thought is to finish with your weight almost 100 percent on your left leg. Only the toe is touching the ground on the right side. Your belt buckle is facing the target. The club, hands and arms finish high above the shoulders.

That full follow-through is important because it will guarantee that you are bringing the club through the rough—that you are not stabbing at the ball. I see many weekenders finish with a weak and halfhearted follow-through. It could be called a semi follow-through.

Those same golfers will make a quick and forceful takeaway. I remind them: Golf does not begin with the takeaway. Golf begins when you are bringing the club down and through.

Drills for Using the Power Swing to Get Out of Trouble

1. To remind yourself how to swing with only the upper gear, as you must do when hitting from a fairway bunker, stand over an imaginary ball with knees and feet close together. Swing a club with both hands. With your feet locked together, you will be swinging with

Swinging with only your right arm, stop the swing when your right shoulder touches your chin.

only the upper gear. Do this 25 times. Use this as a practice swing before you hit a ball out of a fairway bunker.

2. To remind yourself that you must stop the swing at the "shaking hands" position for a punch shot out of

the woods, grip a club with your right hand. Bring the club back, then down and through. Your chin will stop you with your right arm extended at the "shaking hands" position. Do this 25 times to remind your muscle memory that there is no full and high follow-through for the punch shot. As you get ready to take this shot on a course, repeat this exercise three or four times.

3. To remind yourself that you must follow through when hitting from the rough, grip a club with your left hand and take the club back and all the way through, simulating a swing. Do this 25 times to remind yourself that the club must be swept through the rough and up. Do that once or twice as a practice swing whenever you hit from the rough.

Exercises for the Golf Connection

Repeat the drills for Day Five.

Course Management for the Power Golfer

There will be times when you need extra distance with a power swing. You can get that extra distance by shifting to the lower gear. But there will also be situations when the extra distance won't be worth the risk of mishitting the ball and landing in deep trouble.

Let's look at a few typical holes to see when you should stay in upper gear and when you should shift to lower gear.

A Par-3, 185-Yard Hole

Par-3s are the toughest holes to par on a course—any course. A par-3 demands that you hit to the smallest target you will ever aim at from a tee; the green may be no more than 50 feet wide or 50 feet deep. Miss that green and you almost certainly will bogey or double-bogey the hole.

I tell golfers: On par-3s, go for the power club, not the lower-gear super-power swing. In short, stay in upper gear. On this hole, if you usually need a four-iron to cover 185 yards, take a three-iron. The stronger club will make up for the extra distance lost by keeping the upper-gear action in control of the swing. Trust the late wrist release just before impact to give you the distance that you need. And a full follow-through, your left arm acting as the connecting rod, will give you the straight trajectory that you need on a par-3. If you face a head wind on a par-3, I might even suggest going two clubs stronger, in this case choosing a five-wood.

Holding a strong club, tell yourself: "I have ample club to reach the green. In fact, I have more club than I really need. So I will take a slow backswing, a strong downswing that will be faster than my upswing and a full and relaxed through swing. I know I am going to get there—to that pin or close to it—without having to overwork the club."

But when I give this advice, many golfers say to me, "But, Walter, I don't want to drive over the green with that strong a club."

My answer: "How often do you hit a golf ball perfectly?"

Not very often, even low-handicappers will admit. "If you hit that tee shot perfectly with a strong club," I tell them, "you will go over the green. But remember: On most greens the trouble is usually in the front of the green and on the sides, seldom in the back.

"Now suppose, as happens more often than not, you hit the ball less than perfectly. If you used your normal club for this distance, the ball would land short of the green and you would have to pitch or chip; very likely you would not get your par-3. But if you are swinging a stronger club and hit it less than perfectly, you are much more likely to get the distance you need to the green or even to the pin if it's in the center of the green."

My final advice to power golfers on par-3s: Aim for the back of the green, not for the front. Again, if you don't get 100 percent into the shot, the ball may still land on the green if you are shooting for the back of the green. If you aim for the pin or the front of the green and you don't get 100 percent, you are likely to land short.

A Short-to-Medium Par-4 of About 330 to 370 Yards

I see golfers shift to the lower gear and try to smash long tee shots on these holes. They figure that they will then have an easy shot of 110 to 150 yards to the green. That's not good strategic thinking. Your tee shot on these holes should definitely be with upper-gear action. Here's why:

Your main concern is to land the ball in the middle of the fairway. Once you do that, any club in your bag should be strong enough to reach the green—whether a four- or a five-iron from 170 yards away or a nine-iron or a wedge from 110 yards away. So on these short-to-medium-distance holes, you can take a much-less-risky upper-gear swing from the tee and another comfortable upper-gear swing from the fairway for your approach shot.

A Long Par-4 from 370 to 420 Yards

Now here is where you need a long tee shot and a long second shot (and perhaps a short third shot, depending on the hole and your handicap) to reach the green. So you should shift to the lower gear, going for the extra distance from the tee and with your second shot from the fairway. If you can get 225 yards from the tee and another 150 to 200 yards with your second shot, depending on the hole, you will be on the green in regulation. Most weekenders need two lower-gear swings and one upper-gear short-iron shot to get on the longer par-4s in three, but a bogey on a par-4 of this length is something for which you should thank your power swing.

A Par 5 of 450 to 500-Plus Yards

You want to swallow distance on the fairway with your first two or three shots, depending on the length of the hole and your handicap. Then you will have an easy and comfortable third or fourth short-iron approach to the green. So shift down to lower gear for your first two or three shots, and go to upper gear from within a hundred yards.

By now you should be able to cover 400 yards or close to it with a driver and a fairway wood or a long iron. When you don't get 100 percent of the ball, your new power swing will give you 350 yards with two swings more often than not on most holes. That means on most long par-4s and on nearly all par-5s, you will be swinging from within 100 yards of the green for your third or fourth shot. If you can land on the green with a high percentage of your third shots on par-4 greens, and hit the green with a high percentage of your fourth shots on par-5s, you are on your way to being a golfer who shoots in the 80s.

Drill for Course Management

At a practice range, use upper-gear and lower-gear action to hit a bucket of balls with clubs ranging from the driver to the wedge. If you think you average 200 yards with a driver, hit two or three balls with a driver. Make a note of how far the balls actually travel. Do the same with your woods and irons. You now have a better idea of what your average distance is with each club.

Exercises for the Golf Connection

Repeat the exercises for Day One.

At the Pro Shop: Equipment for Power Golf

The clubs you have been swinging—and the balls you have been hitting—may not be the right ones for your new power-golf swing. Or they might be just fine. Let's find out by looking at golf clubs and golf balls.

CLUBS

Most golfers who want to hit for distance carry a set of woods that include the number one, three and five, matched with a utility high-lofted club, such as a number seven digging wood; a seven-wood will get you out of deep rough. Iron sets usually include the number three, four, five, six, seven, eight, nine, a pitching wedge and a sand wedge.

The shafts of clubs vary considerably as far as flexibility is concerned. You can buy shafts that are almost as flexible as buggy whips, while others are almost as rigid as flagpoles. When you swing a club with a very flexible shaft, the clubhead is always going to be lagging behind the hands as you enter the Impact Zone. Obviously, then, the power swinger should be looking for clubs with very little flex. The stronger the swing, the firmer the shaft should be. A PGA teaching pro—you'll find one at any club or public course—can advise you, after watching you swing, what the right shaft flex is for you.

Club shafts are made of stainless steel, graphite or titanium. Graphite and titanium shafts have become very popular—even though they are more expensive than steel shafts—because they are lighter and thus will give you more clubhead speed. They come in all degrees of flexibility.

To my mind, however, steel shafts are the best choice for weekend power hitters. It's true that if you make a perfect swing, you are going to get super-distance with titanium or graphite shafts—distance you won't get with a steel shaft. But if you impact the ball slightly off target with all that clubhead speed, the titanium and graphite shafts will magnify the mistake. You end up in the woods, while the same mis-hit with a steel shaft might put you only in the rough. Most weekend power hitters want as much consistency as possible in their game. Stainless-steel shafts will give you more consistency than titanium or graphite.

You've heard talk, I know, about swing weight, which refers mostly to the weight of the clubhead. Until recent years, designers were making heads extremely light, so that even those so-called 119-pound "weaklings" could build up clubhead speed. But those light clubheads lacked the weight that told you where you were in the swing. In recent years, the manufacturers have gone back to heavier heads.

Swing weights come in three classes: heavy, medium and light. Most men who want to hit long should swing medium-weight woods and irons. Again, you should consult with a golf pro, who will recommend the right swing weight for your build and swing. Most men should use a D-1 or D-2 swing weight, most women C-5, C-6 or C-7.

Clubheads of drivers vary in their degree of loft or pitch. My driver's pitch is 10 degrees, but some of you might have trouble getting the ball airborne with that straight a clubface. Obviously, though, the straighter the clubface, the more line drives you can hit, the ones with overspin that roll and roll and roll. The more lofted the driver, the more fly balls you are going to hit. They come down vertically and stop quickly. But you are more likely to get the ball up into the air with a lofted driver than with a straighter club.

With your new power swing, you will be able to go for more distance with a driver with 11 or 12 degrees of loft. The ball will go up a little higher than a club with less loft. But the more loft, the more forgiving the club. And aggressive swingers, as I have warned you, are often in need of forgiveness.

The "Jumbo," or oversize, drivers have become immensely popular. The larger heads are as much as 30 percent bigger than the usual heads—yet they often are lighter.

Some golfers hit longer and straighter with Jumbo heads simply because the head looks bigger. That huge head gives golfers more confidence that they will make contact with the ball.

Also, because the head is bigger, the center of gravity is moved back toward the rear of the head. That helps the golfer get the ball airborne because there is more

The larger heads of Jumbo drivers (*top*) are as much as 30 percent bigger than the usual heads.

margin of error. And once you have the confidence that you will make contact and get the ball up into the air, you are much more likely to continue the swing into a high and full follow-through. As you have seen in the lessons so far, it is the momentum of the follow-through—that straight left arm or connecting rod—that guarantees both distance and accuracy.

So Jumbo heads, I have found, are what you should buy if you lack confidence in your driving. They psych you into believing you will make contact; they psych you into believing you will get the ball airborne; and they psych you into a full and high follow-through. Indeed, you might say that the big advantage of the Jumbo head is all in the head.

One final tip on clubs: Since you will be taking a power swing with a high upswing that brings the clubhead at least parallel to the ground, don't lose your grip on the club. That often happens at the top of the backswing. To prevent this, your grips should be made a little thicker so your hands and fingers fit on them more firmly. Any pro shop can replace your old grips with oversize grips.

BALLS

There are three different kinds of golf balls. There are solid, or two-piece, balls, the two pieces being a core and a cover; there are wound balls, made with a core, windings around the core and a cover; and there are three-piece balls, which are built with a big core, some winding and a cover.

The covers are either made of balata, a natural rubber, or a synthetic material called Surlyn. The balata balls cut more easily than Surlyn balls, but most pros prefer the balata ball because it has a softer "feel" when struck by a club.

Golf balls also vary in compression. Golf balls come in 80, 90 and 100 compressions. To understand compression, visualize a beach ball that has very little air in it. If you kick the ball, your foot will flatten one side of the ball—the side of the ball that you kicked. You compressed it. But a near airless ball won't fly very far. If you fill the ball with air, you will have to kick it hard to compress, or flatten the ball at the point where you kicked it. But you know that the ball filled with air will fly much farther than the ball with little or no air in it.

Now let's get one thing straight: Golf balls are not filled with air. But their innards are compressed just as air is compressed inside a beach ball. The higher the compression of a golf ball, the more clubhead impact or force is needed to flatten the side of the ball and make it go; just as the more air there is in a beach ball, the harder you have to kick it to flatten its side.

But when you flatten that side, the highly compressed ball's response—its kickback—is greater. Therefore, the ball flies farther than a ball with little compression (because there is less response or kickback from a low-compression ball).

Now let's see what all this has to do with your swing and the compression of your golf ball. If you have a swing that is of medium force and medium speed, you should use a 90 compression ball. That's because only medium force is needed to flatten the side of the ball—and thus get a kickback that will make the ball fly. But like the beach ball that is only 90 percent filled with air, the beach ball will not go as far as a beach ball that is 100 percent filled with air.

Now, with your new power swing, you are bringing the club down with more force. You should try the 100 compression ball. You should be able to flatten it and get the response, or kickback, that the 100 compression ball gives you—extra yards.

Most weekenders should use a ball with a Surlyn cover because they cut less easily than balata balls. And I recommend that weekenders use one of the solid balls—Top Flite, Pinnacle and Ultra are the most popular. The solid balls ride through the air with overspin that keeps the ball rolling after it lands. The wound balls get airborne more easily, but they ride through the air with backspin and stop more quickly. In an ideal world, we'd tee off with a solid ball that would roll on the fairway; then we'd switch to a wound ball for an approach shot that would stick to the green. Unfortunately, switching balls on a hole is against the rules.

GLOVES

Finally, let's look at an underrated piece of golf equipment—the glove. I tell all weekenders: "Wear a glove!" And not just for aesthetic reasons, such as sparing your hands from unsightly blisters or calluses. The glove connects your hands and fingers to the club and helps to make sure that they stay connected. With a power swing, you bring the club's shaft parallel to the ground at the top of the upswing; you may even dip the clubhead toward the ground. That's the point where weekenders often lose their grip on the club. If the clubhead turns, a mis-hit is almost a sure thing. A glove will help to keep the grip firm from upswing to follow-through.

The glove can also be a mental reminder, since we wear it on the left hand, that the left hand and the left arm are the dominant ones in a right-hander's golf swing.

Gloves come in synthetic materials that feel like leather, or there are more expensive leather gloves. Whatever the glove's material, make sure that the glove fits smoothly and securely. If in doubt, consult a PGA teaching pro.

In fact, I'll conclude this lesson by saying that you should consult with a PGA teaching pro before you buy any golf equipment or clothing. A pro, for example, will tell you that you should buy a golf shirt that's a little big for you, since a tight shirt can constrict your swing. You need that kind of professional advice, since none of us is built the same nor do we swing exactly the same. A PGA or LPGA teaching pro has spent a good part of his or her life learning how to fit golfers with the appropriate equipment. Buying clubs in a store from salespeople who may never have picked up a golf club in their lives . . . well, to me, that's about as smart as taking driving lessons from someone who doesn't drive.

Exercises for the Golf Connection

Repeat the exercises for Day Six.

DAY FOURTEEN

How to Practice for Power

Ideally, what you want to get from a practice session at a driving range is a swing that produces long and accurate shots—a swing that you can bring to the golf course the next time you play a round.

That's the ideal. That's not easy to do when you have time to hit only a bucket of balls in a half hour. But if you go to a driving range with the notion that your driving-range game is also your golf-course game, you can leave the range ready to perform on a golf course what you have just accomplished at the range.

Most weekenders just belt balls when they go to a driving range. If they hit one ball 250 yards, they go away happy. They forget about the hooked shots, the sliced shots, the topped shots.

They would not leave a golf course happy if they had hit only one ball 250 yards and had sliced, hooked or topped every other ball. Yet you must make your golf-course game an extension of your driving-range game. You never want to leave your good swing back on the driving range. They don't count strokes on a driving range.

I tell golfers that there are four different segments that make up a successful practice session at a driving range:

The first segment: Five or ten minutes of practice swinging with each of two or three clubs at an imaginary ball. Check your basics: grip; stance; alignment of the feet, knees and shoulders with the target line; a slow upswing; an aggressive downswing; straightening of the wrists just before impact; a nice V-shaped formation of the arms at impact and a full and high follow-through.

The second segment: Hit 15 golf balls with each of the two or three clubs to loosen up and stretch the muscles. Make sure that all the pieces of the swing are coming together in the proper sequence from takeaway to follow-through. Don't worry about where the ball goes; you are simply trying to get the feel of a comfortable swing.

The third segment: With the next 15 balls, work on the tempo of your swing. Start with an upswing of 30 miles an hour and a downswing of 30 miles an hour. After hitting three or four balls, swing a little more aggressively on the downswing—the way you would swing on a golf course.

We all swing more aggressively on a course than on the range. On a course there is a distant green to reach, a fairway bunker to go over and hazards and other situations that we don't face on the range. So, on the course, we swing a little harder. But on the range we want to simulate the golf-course swing. Step up the force of your downswing with each of the three clubs. I don't mean you should be swinging for the fences, but you should be swinging close to the downswing speed you would use on a course.

If the balls are going straight, turn up the volume. Come down to impact even faster. If you hook or slice, turn down the volume until you are hitting the ball straight or, at least, straighter. Find your speed limit.

The fourth segment: With the last 10 balls in the bucket, hit two or three with each club, aiming for a target. It should be a target such as a flag or a marker that is the same distance from you as your average distance with the club. If you can hit a five-iron 150 yards, aim for a target 150 yards away. Give yourself a tolerance of about 10 yards on either side of the target. Thus, if you were aiming for the pin on a green on a golf course, you would land on that green no more than 10 yards to the left or right of the pin.

In short, as your practice session comes to an end, you have gone from a driving-range situation to a golf-course situation. Each of these last ten swings counts. Five of the 10 balls should land within the target area. That would be "par"; you have had a successful practice session. If you drop more than five of the 10 balls within the target area, that's a "birdie"; you have had a super successful practice session. If fewer than five balls land within the target area, maybe you should come back tomorrow.

Drill for Power-Swing Practicing

Going to and from a driving range will probably take more time than the hour you practice at the range. But a driving range is not the only place you can practice.

You can hit plastic balls in your backyard—or almost anywhere else indoors or outdoors. Buy 40 or 50 plastic balls and go through the four segments of a worthwhile one-hour practice session.

Exercises for the Golf Connection

Repeat the exercises for Day Six.

The Keys to Power Golf

It is eight o'clock in the morning. You are teeing off at 8:30 to play your first round of power golf. I can't walk around the course with you, but I can give you this last lesson that should get you ready to swing for distance plus.

First, take a few swings at an imaginary ball with any club that you are comfortable with. You are getting the muscles and the mind thinking about golf—and only golf.

As you swing at the imaginary ball, go through the checkpoints of your swing. Make sure that your grip is comfortable. You are not oversqueezing the club, but it should feel secure.

As you take the club away, remind yourself of the two keys to a good upswing: (1) It is slow and deliberate, and (2) your weight moves in the direction the club is moving—away from you. Thus your weight is now mostly on your right leg. Make sure that you point your left knee and left shoulder toward the ball. When you feel your left shoulder touch your chin, you know you have completed your takeaway.

Now make your down and through swing, coming

down at about twice the speed with which you brought up the club. Your important checkpoints are to make sure that hands and wrists begin to straighten as the clubhead passes your right hip, and that your arms and hands form the same V pattern at impact that they formed at address.

Finally, finish with arms and hands and club over your shoulders in a nice, easy fashion on the other side of the swing. Remind yourself of a final key: Make sure the ends match up. If you took the club back to where the shaft was parallel to the ground, bring the club around in the follow-through to where the clubhead is at least parallel to the ground.

Do six to eight easy to moderately paced rehearsal swings—no ball. Then swing with live ammunition—with a ball. And swing with a comfortable club. I usually pick the six-iron, because it is the perfect length—not a long club nor a short club—but right in the middle.

Make three or four swings that are upper-gear dominant, using primarily the shoulders, arms and hands. Concentrate on two points: left shoulder touching the chin on the upswing, right shoulder touching the chin on the through swing. Aim to knock at least one ball into a target area that's the right distance for the club, in my case about 150 yards with a six-iron.

Now shift down to the lower gear for the super power swing. Remind yourself of key points: Bring up the clubhead slowly, making sure the shoulder turn completes itself and that the club gets into a high position and that your weight goes from in balance to out of balance, most of it on your right leg. As you bring down the club, get your weight over to your left leg, which takes you out of balance on the left side. As your hands come down to between the waist and the right knee, start to straighten your wrists so that the clubhead becomes as square to the ball at impact as it was at address. The clubhead catches up with the left hip and passes the left hip after impact. As your right knee turns to face the ball, your hands, clubhead and legs produce a slingshot effect. Result: more clubhead speed than with the upper-gear power swing.

Finally, my last key is to keep your left arm straight until it passes your belt buckle, so that the clubhead is forced to stay on the line of flight.

Now you are ready to go out there and play an aggressive round of golf. Be willing to accept some wild shots that will veer to the left or right, but also tell yourself that you will go back to my keys, especially the one reminding you to keep the left arm straight at impact and into the follow-through—the connecting rod. By keeping that left arm straight, you will hit fewer slices and hooks and more balls that go long and straight to the target.

And I assure you as you head out for your first round of power golf: With these 15 lessons and the drills and exercises I have given you, you can play power golf.

You are ready, so let's do it!

Exercises for the Golf Connection

Pick four of the exercises that I have given during the past 15 days. Do at least two of the exercises for a total of 30 minutes each day. Remember: You must supply the power to the club for the club to do its job—and the only way you can supply that power to the club is through your Golf Connection—hands, wrists and arms.

About the Authors

Walter Ostroske has been a PGA teaching pro for the past 25 years. He has played in numerous tournaments and has written magazine articles on golf instruction. Currently head pro at the Hempstead Golf and Country Club on Long Island, he is a member of the MacGregor Advisory Staff.

John Devaney is the author of more than 25 books and has written hundreds of magazine articles on sports. The former editor of *Sport Magazine*, he is the editor of Harris Publications golf magazines and is an adjunct lecturer at Fordham University.

Walter Ostroske and John Devaney are the authors of the highly successful *Break 100 in 21 Days: A How-to Guide for the Weekend Golfer, Correct the 10 Most Common Golf Problems in 10 Days* and *Two-Putt Greens in 18 Days: A How-to Guide for the Weekend Golfer*.

ABOUT THE PHOTOGRAPHER

Aime J. LaMontagne is a successful free-lance photographer living in Palmer, Massachusetts. His golfing photographs have appeared in national magazines.

More power to you, from (*left to right*): Aime LaMontagne, Walter Ostroske, John Devaney.

Improve your game with these comprehensive Perigee golf guides.

Break 100 in 21 Days
A How-to Guide for the Weekend Golfer
by Walter Ostroske and John Devaney
illustrated with over 50 black-and-white photographs
The first easy-to-follow program by a PGA teaching pro for shooting in the 90s and 80s, aimed at the person who plays only ten to twenty times a year.

Correct the 10 Most Common Golf Problems in 10 Days
by Walter Ostroske and John Devaney
illustrated with over 50 black-and-white photographs
The first book to pinpoint and correct the ten most common problems in golfers' swings—in just ten days.

Golf Games Within the Game
200 Fun Ways Players Can Add Variety and Challenge to Their Game
by Linda Valentine and Margie Hubbard
illustrated with over 25 line drawings
A one-of-a-kind collection of games and bets for added excitement on the golf course, culled from members of more than 8,000 golf clubs across America.

Golf Rules in Pictures
An Official Publication of the United States Golf Association
introduction by Arnold Palmer
Clearly captioned pictures cover all the rules of golf: scoring, clubs, procedure, hazards, and penalty strokes. Includes the official text of the Rules of Golf approved by the U.S. Golf Association and the Royal and Ancient Golf Club of St. Andrews, Scotland.

Golf Techniques in Pictures
by Michael Brown
illustrated with over 100 line drawings
Chock-full of both fundamental and advanced techniques, this is the most complete handbook for successful swinging, putting, and chipping.

Power Swing in 15 Days
A How-to Guide for the Weekend Golfer
by Walter Ostroske and John Devaney
illustrated with over 50 black-and-white photographs
Will teach any golfer to hit up to 200 yards or more in just fifteen days.

Two-Putt Greens in 18 Days
A How-to Guide for the Weekend Golfer
by Walter Ostroske and John Devaney
illustrated with over 50 black-and-white photographs
An easy-to-use daily program for mastering good putting in just eighteen days.

These books are available at your local bookstore or wherever books are sold. Ordering is also easy and convenient. Just call 1-800-631-8571 or send your order to:

The Putnam Publishing Group
390 Murray Hill Parkway, Dept. B
East Rutherford, NJ 07073

		U.S.	CAN
___ Break 100 in 21 Days	399-51600-X	$8.95	$11.75
___ Correct the 10 Most Common Golf Problems in 10 Days	399-51656-5	8.95	11.75
___ Golf Games Within the Game	399-51762-6	8.95	11.75
___ Golf Rules in Pictures	399-51799-5	7.95	10.50
___ Golf Techniques in Pictures	399-51664-6	7.95	10.50
___ Power Swing in 15 Days	399-51797-9	8.95	11.75
___ Two-Putt Greens in 18 Days	399-51747-2	8.95	11.75

Subtotal $_____

Postage and handling* $_____

Sales tax (CA, NJ, NY, PA, Canada) $_____

Total Amount Due $_____

Payable in U.S. funds (no cash orders accepted). $15.00 minimum for credit card orders.
*Postage and handling: $2.50 for 1 book, 75¢ for each additional book up to a maximum of $6.25.

Enclosed is my ☐ check ☐ money order
Please charge my ☐ Visa ☐ MasterCard ☐ American Express

Card # _____ Expiration date _____

Signature as on charge card _____

Name _____

Address _____

City _____ State _____ Zip _____

Please allow six weeks for delivery. Prices subject to change without notice.

Source Key #19